AF413130

Exploring Psychology

THREE ESSAYS

by

Roberta Provenzano, Ph. D

Gotham Books

30 N Gould St.
Ste. 20820, Sheridan, WY 82801
https://gothambooksinc.com/

Phone: 1 (307) 464-7800

Published by Gotham Books (June 16, 2023)

ISBN: 979-8-88775-340-9 H
ISBN: 979-8-88775-338-6 P
ISBN: 979-8-88775-339-3 E

Because of the dynamic nature of the Internet, any web addresses or links contained in this book may have changed since publication and may no longer be valid.

The views expressed in this work are solely those of the author and do not necessarily reflect the views of the publisher, and the publisher hereby disclaims any responsibility for them.

CONTENTS

This set of essays, divided into three thematic sections: Psychology as the *Study of the Soul*, Psychology as the *Science of Consciousness*, and Psychology as a *Human Science*, means to highlight three stages in the evolution of psychology, from the times when it was not yet a separate discipline but was part of philosophy, to the modern era where it has become an independent, scientific study of the mind and behavior.

Written in an easy-to-grasp manner, they are intended to give a concise overview of the evolution of psychology and to capture the interest of readers versed or not in this field. The three essays are a posthumous publication of Roberta Provenzano, Ph.D., assembled and edited by Carmen Barthet, Friend, and legal representative.

Provenzano said that psychology cannot be limited to behaviorism or psychoanalysis, and must be holistic, finding its place in the "Second Copernican Revolution", bringing more wisdom and happiness to this world".

Behaviorism, a materialistic system which denies the reality of mind and consciousness, is not dealt with in this review. Behaviorists affirm that if psychology is to be a science at all, it must follow the patterns of physical sciences, that is conform to the materialistic, mechanistic, objective mold. This is the very position of the famous Behaviorist B.F. Skinner, for whom free will is inexistent. However, though she disagreed with his theory, Roberta admired him as an outstanding and fascinating scholar and loved to meet him and attend his lectures at the APA conventions, as shown on the signed picture below.

New York, 8 November 2022

____

The latest WORD on Behaviorism

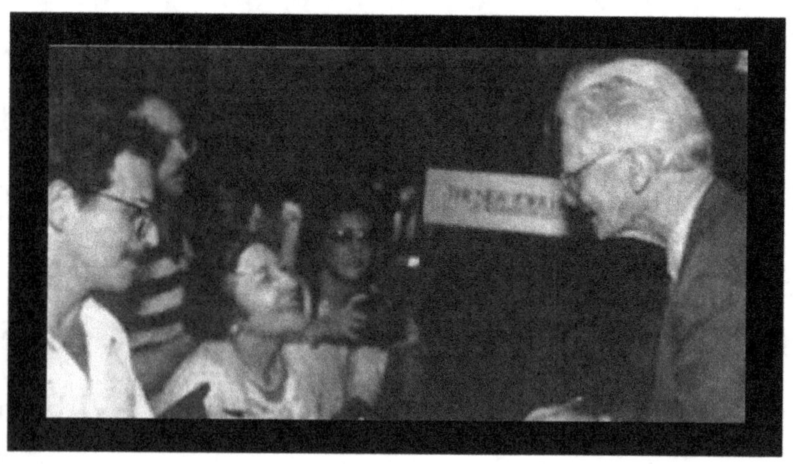

B.F. Skinner chats with admirers

INTRODUCTION

The present essays are meant to emphasize what makes psychology a study of the mind, with its own approach, scientific experimental methods, and unique interpretation linked to either materialistic, humanistic, or spiritualistic dimensions of reality.

Starting at the beginning, that is with Greek philosophy, this presentation proposes first an oversight of Platonism and Aristotelianism, the two most prominent philosophic currents that have shaped Western civilization since Antiquity, providing however two sensibly different and even opposed concepts of reality.

Within his idealistic and dualistic system, Plato (427-347 B.C.) formulated a clear distinction between mind and matter, a position that has endured till the present time.

Another tenet of Plato's metaphysics, logically related to the mind/matter dichotomy, is the opposition between ideas conceived by reason, and things perceived by the senses. In Plato's metaphysics, ideas have a perfection that is never present in concrete things, and remain unchanged, even when the sense objects which they reflect disappear. To Plato, it seems evident that the permanent, the perfect, the changeless, and the absolute inherent to ideas are more real than the perishable, inconstant, imperfect objects.

The world revealed by the senses is only a shadow of the realm of ideas 1 *.

To Plato rationality rests on a priori, or self-evident axioms, such as used in syllogisms or deductive reasoning, proceeding from general statements to particulars.

The main component in Plato's metaphysics is the concept of the soul. The soul, or principle of life integrates three elements: desire, will, and thought, each with its own virtue – moderation, courage, and wisdom.

The soul is the self-moving force in man, and part of the self-moving soul of all things. It is pure vitality, incorporated, and immortal. It existed before temporarily dwelling in the body.

Then comes an overview of Aristotle (384-322 B.C) who states that psychology is « the study of the soul », as specifically embodied in his major work De anima (« on the soul »). For Aristotle, the soul had two aspects, a mortal, and an immortal. The mortal aspect is connected to the functions of bodily structures that perish at death, while the immaterial aspect connected to the intellect is immortal.

Aristotle agrees with Plato that the deductive method is the only acceptable one; however, there is a crucial difference between Plato and Aristotle on how to arrive at the first principles. The first principles for Aristotle are derived from experience. Rationality thus involves a necessary empirical or experimental element. He, therefore, dismisses the platonic concept of arriving at first principles through a priori methods.

He states in Metaphysics that knowledge is inevitably rooted in sense experiences, and that ultimate knowledge has to do with individual objects of experience.

Aristotle is said to be the founder of the scientific method and in his « Life of Jesus » Ernest Renan wrote « Socrates gave philosophy to mankind and Aristotle gave it science »

---

* This assertion is strangely echoing a statement made some 400 years later by St Paul in 2 Corinthians 4:18 : « … *because we look not to the things that are seen but to the things that are unseen, for the things that are seen are transient, but the things that are unseen are eternal* ».

The Christian era is then explored. Christian philosophy concentrated on the moral aspects of human life, on man's relation to God. The towering figure among the Fathers of the Catholic Church, was St Augustine (354-430 A.D.). His autobiography « The Confessions » gained him the title of modern psychologist » because in it he presented a penetrating and sincere self-analysis of his own emotions, thoughts, memories, and motives. These inner experiences a modern man can easily understand despite a lapse of fifteen centuries. This is what makes the Confessions, a unique work of self-analysis in which Augustine goes deeper into his own character and deeds, passes keen judgments upon himself, and reveals himself fully and humbly to others.

Then, the seventeenth century brings a definite change in the treatment of psychology. Observation and induction now supplant metaphysical analysis and deduction. Psychology decidedly ceases to be the science of the soul. Instead, the mind and its operations become the main interest, and psychology is viewed as the science of consciousness, opening the road to scientific, experimental psychology.

After Descartes, the Empirical school (1588-1776) initiated a radical change in psychological thought, holding that experience is the sole source of knowledge. Advances in experimental psychology culminated in the establishment of systems like structuralism and Functionalism, associated with famous names such as Wundt, James, Fechner, Titchener.

In the third part, psychology is presented as a human science. It recapitulates the historical progression as follows: « Historically psychology has begun as the 'science of the soul', when all is explained by the existence of a Supreme value outside of man. This concept is later discarded in favor of a 'science of consciousness' explained in practical terms when psychology breaks from philosophy. The scientific method applied to this science of consciousness is then found inadequate if psychology is to fulfill its intrinsic potential, and some scholars believe that psychology ought to be a human science, or at least different from the natural sciences. This section focuses on Carl Jung, seen as a pioneer of humanistic psychology through the expansion of consciousness, even crossing the threshold into spiritual psychology.

PSYCHOLOGY

AS THE

Study of the Soul

The earliest traces of psychological thought in the Western world are to be found in ancient Greek philosophy – which then embraced all fields of knowledge – and in medicine. The Greek approach to the fundamental problems of modern psychology (sensation, perception, learning and memory, emotions, motivation, sleep, and dreams, etc.,) was sometimes physiological or biological and based on observations, and sometimes metaphysical.

Plato (427-347 B.C.)

Influenced by Socrates' admonishment to care for the soul, was the first of the Greek thinkers to develop a philosophical system which was idealistic, spiritualistic, and dualistic, and to differentiate between the spiritual world and the material world. From the distinction between the two levels of man's knowledge – the sensory and the intellectual – and

also because of Pythagorean influence, Plato derived the concept of the human soul. To him the soul was a complete substance, of divine origin, spiritual, immortal, and eternal. It lived independently before coming to dwell in the body. It is imprisoned by the body, but only temporarily until the body's death.

Plato also formed the first clearly defined concept of immaterial existence and posited that the immaterial world consists of "Ideas". According to him, ideas were the eternal reality of the universe; they were absolute forms or models of which all earthly objects were nothing but incomplete reflections.

The philosophy of Plato affirms that ideas are the only reality, although in animals and young children the Ideas are thoroughly confused with matter. In adult humans, the Ideas gradually regain their freedom from matter and become the "Psyche" or rational soul. It is the Psyche that generates mental activity and produces intuitive knowledge.

Plato adopted the Sophists theory of sensations, stating that sensations occur when the activity of external objects unites with the activity of the sense organs. He disagreed, however, with the thesis that all knowledge originates in experience and sensation, since he advocated that knowledge was the result of solely innate Ideas.

Sensations, according to Plato, only provided the necessary stimulus to arouse the "reminiscence" of Ideas in the Psyche.

But for all his brilliant journeys through so many different aspects of psychological matters, Plato always approached these ideas from a non-psychological position. It was his famous disciple Aristotle who developed the first complete system of psychology in De Anima and who may therefore be regarded as the first philosophical psychologist.

Aristotle (384-322)

Although Aristotle began sharing Plato's views, he later opposed the Platonic idealist tradition. He introduced physiological and biological observations to Plato's metaphysical construct of the Psyche.

Aristotle's treatment of psychology is intimately connected with his study of biology, although he defined psychology as "the study of the soul". Mind, according to him, is a part of nature. Aristotle posited that nature is arranged in an evolutionary scale in which each object is "form" for the next lower stage and is "matter" for the next higher stage. The "form" activity he named "entelechy". In his psychology the Psyche is the entelechy (form) of the entire organism.

Aristotle distinguished three levels of the activity of the Psyche:
(a) The lowest is the vegetative soul as is possessed by plants.

b) The middle one is the sensitive or sensory soul as is possessed by animals.

c) Human beings possess a higher development of the two lower stages, the rational soul. The only metaphysical element in Aristotle's otherwise perfectly biological psychology is his concept of "active reason", the very highest form of reason, which is considered transcendental and immortal.

Aristotle's biologism proposes that the heart is the central seat of life, motion, and sensation. The heart produces a mixture of blood and air called the "pneuma". The pneuma mediates between sense impressions and the heart. Sense impressions result from the motion of objects. The senses furnish all the knowledge that man possesses. Memories of past experiences are aroused by the heart which stirs up the pneuma and revives the traces of past impressions in the sense organs.

Reason is the highest activity of the Psyche. Bodily activities are controlled by the heart by means of the Psyche. The Psyche always acts in reference to something.

After Aristotle's death, which marks the close of the most original and productive period in Greek thought, there was no other original and productive period in Greek thought, there was no other original system of psychology in the ancient world, although much psychological material was to be found in the writings of Greek and Roman philosophers.

Among the philosophies that flourished in that era, the views held by the Stoics and the Epicureans are the most interesting to psychology because of the contrasting attitudes they took in their practical life.

Both schools were only concerned with making the most of human life: the Stoics by standing for suppression, and the Epicureans for expression of natural impulses. Theirs was indeed a practical application of psychology in their everyday living and they were more preoccupied with developing systems of practical ethics than they were concerned with producing a theoretical-scientific psychology.

The Christian era marks the point of return to psychology into ethics before it would be completely absorbed by religion. Psychological theory, much like philosophical theory, in this period regresses to an almost pre-philosophical simplicity, as Christian philosophy concentrates on the religious and moral aspects of human life.

The Christian authors of the first seven centuries – called Fathers of the Church – and later, the Christian theologians and philosophers, were principally concerned with the spiritual nature of the soul, man's relation to God, and his eternal salvation. The psychological processes as such were of secondary interest to them.

However, the Church Fathers wrote frequently and analytically about man's inner experiences, spiritual development, and behavior, his thoughts, memories, emotions, and motives. These inner experiences, which are inherent in man still ring true to modern man after a span of fifteen centuries.

St. Augustine (354-430)

The chief representative of the Church Fathers, St. Augustine, (354-430) made the first use of introspection as a definite method of investigation in his famous autobiography, the Confessions, which won him the title of "First modern psychologist" as this literary masterpiece he recounts the dramatic and exciting story of a human soul in search of God, presenting a penetrating and sincere analysis of his own experiences, desires, thoughts, and feelings.

Augustine, who was born in North Africa at Tagasts, near Tripoli, when the Huns began their migration westward from Mongolia and started pouring into the Roman empire, and died during the fourteen-month siege of Hippo by the Vandals, lived during the twilight of the Western Roman empire.

The fourth century marked the official death of paganism as well as the growth of the Catholic Church that was to spread its power over a third of Europe by the twelfth century.

Some Christian writers often refer to the fact that Aquinas is the Christian Aristotle and Augustine the Christian Plato. It is evident that both borrowed liberally from these Greek thinkers. In Augustine's case, Plato is described with the adulation of an admirer and follower. Since Augustine had never mastered Greek, it is highly probable that he achieved his knowledge of Plato through the interpretations of the immensely popular Neo-Platonists of his time.

His contact with Neo-Platonism profoundly moved him. When he began reading Plotinus (205-270) he discovered in this philosophy a means by which he might explain the phenomena of materiality in spiritual terms, as well as account for the problem of evil in the concept of negation rather than the dualism of the ancient Manichean view in which he believed.

The Manicheans taught that there existed two ultimate principles of reality in a state of constant warfare: God, the principle of light, or forces of good, and Satan, the principle of darkness, or forces of evil. Man finds himself subject to the principle of darkness and must free himself by acts of extreme asceticism, denying himself the pleasures of the flesh, because whatever proceeds from the body results from the workings of the principle of evil and is in continual conflict with the effects of the soul that comes from God, or the principle of light.

Augustine's rejection of Manichaeism led the way to his favorable reception of the doctrine of Christianity and ultimately to his conversion, which culminated in the establishment of a small monastic community that was to grow into the present-day religious order of Augustinians, numbering Martin Luther among some of its more renowned members.

About a century before the birth of Augustine, the philosophical school created by Amonius Saccas at Alexandria in Egypt established the beginnings of Neo-Platonic philosophy. Plotinus studied there for ten years and became the most eloquent and influential spokesman for this system of thought. He provided an interesting adaptation of Plato's Timaeus, along with the essential elements of objective idealism, to a quasi-religious interpretation of the universe.

This philosophy proposed the idea that God was universally one, existing in three conditions of being. Fundamentally, being in itself can never be known by man because it is the ground of all reality in its most abstract and spiritual form. The Nous is the eternal world-mind which emanates from being in itself. There exist two world souls which stand in relationship to the Nous. One has no immediate contact with material reality, and the other represents a lesser form which constitutes the ideas which are the reality of phenomenal existence.

Matter is the lowest level of existence. Plotinus views matter as the absence of spirit. It is the source of evil therefore, and evil is merely the absence of spiritual being. The idea that God is transcendent and loses nothing by this emanation which possesses individual reality, saves Neo-Platonism from pure pantheism. It takes an anti-intellectual approach towards understanding God.

Plotinus asserted continuously that no predicates could be attributed to God who is unknowable.

The central theme of Plotinus' teaching is then mystical reunion with the first world soul, as he describes it in the *Six Enneads:*

"But there are earlier and loftier beauties than these. In the sense-bound life we are no longer granted to know them, but the soul, taking no help from the organs, sees and proclaims them. To the vision of these, we must mount, leaving sense to its own low place".

He is even more explicit in a letter written around 260 to his disciple Flaccus, where he states that *"Knowledge has three degrees: opinion, science, illumination". The mystical experience is the only way to know the Infinite which cannot be captured through reason alone. "You can only apprehend the Infinite by a faculty superior to reason, by entering into a state in which you are your finite self no longer – in which the divine essence is communicated to you. This is ecstasy.*

It is the liberation of your mind from its finite consciousness. Like only can apprehend like; when you thus, cease to be finite, you become one with the Infinite. In the reduction of your soul to its simplest self, its divine essence, you realize this union – this identity."

[quoted from R. Bucke's Cosmic Consciousness]

Some features of the psychology of Augustine:
Self-existence

Anticipating the seventeenth-century French philosopher Descartes (1596-1650), Augustine begins his theory of knowledge from individual thought: "If I am deceived, I exist".

Man is able to assert his own reality from the act of thinking. His own mental state is beyond doubt and therefore his existence is a certainty.

Because we know objects beyond our minds through the medium of the senses, our knowledge is more or less probable depending upon the reliability of our judgment. The very fact that we admit the existence of probability suggests and proves that absolute certainty exists. The mind knows the external world only indirectly, but it directly knows awareness of self and produces its experience from within the self.

The automatic functions of the body, considered lower, are therefore not part of this self, but are negligible and can safely be discarded.

Absolute truth, however, exists only in God, the source of all ideas. God may choose to give man knowledge of the truth by illuminating man's mind. It is impossible for man ever to achieve knowledge of truth by means of his unaided reason. He must accept the authority of God. With this act of faith in God, man is enabled to arrive at absolute truth due to the presence of God in his soul. The closer man draws to God, the greater becomes his knowledge and therefore wisdom. This truth is indestructible. Augustine reasoned that the indestructibility of truth residing in man's soul proved that the soul was itself indestructible.

Time

Augustine is philosophically and psychologically important for his subjective view of time.

Time is not eternal but rather something created by God at the moment God created the universe and has no reality apart from created existence. There exists a past, identified with memory, a present, and a future, identified with expectation because there are limited material bodies that constitute a frame of reference for the measure of duration. However, there is no time in eternity. Everything is present in the eternal moment with God. There is no beginning and no end in God. Time, therefore, is not of the external world but is an inner experience: time is phenomenological.

<u>*Unity of Mind*</u>

The two major faculties that Augustine attributes to mind are will and reason. Although man's intellect is important in the choice of objects, it is the will which is supreme. The human will move man to reason. It is the will that determines the act by which one chooses to believe. Man must will the act of faith. This emphasis will determine the ethical and moral position of Augustine.

As reason is the result of the intellect, the act of love proceeds from the human will. Man's chief duty and responsibility is to love God. On earth, man must follow the duty of loving God through the observance of God's precepts. Love, then, is the foundation of morality and ethical behavior. Emotions are not restrained by reason but by the law of God, which is the law of love. It is in this love for God that man's love for his fellow man and for himself arises.

In psychological matters Augustine's interest in the inner man derived from his own experience and in this great classic of self-analysis, he brilliantly and insightfully illustrates that when a man becomes aware of difficulties within himself, he turns to reflection. "Turn into yourself: truth dwells inside man".

When the Confessions was first published, about the year 400, Augustine had been the Bishop of Hippo for nearly five years. Rarely had any religious leader spoken so candidly and honestly of his personal life and no writer ever went deeper into his own character and deeds, passed keener judgments upon himself, or revealed himself more fully and humbly to others, with such a wealth of thought and feeling as did Augustine.

The Confessions, therefore, is not only a unique document for understanding the spiritual and ascetical life, and a storehouse of thought for the philosopher and the theologian, but it is also a most penetrating psychological study, written by a man who had great emotional powers along with great powers of intellect and will, who had lived a life of conscious depravity as a quasi-pagan and had turned to a life of austerity as a Catholic.

Augustine is not proud of his youthful immorality. He does not boast of his early indiscretions but describes his life with humility in order to demonstrate his profound indebtedness to the benevolent God. He believes that man can never earn the gift of faith. This represents a gratuitous favor given directly by God to man. Man is sinful by reason of the original sin of Adam and Eve. Nothing that man does can possibly save him from eternal damnation unless the grace earned by the redemption of Christ is given to man by God. His work thus is not only a confession of sins but also a confession of faith and a confession of praise of God.

This is a case history, without parallel in psychology, of a soul as it travels the purgative way, the illuminative way, and the unitive way, which could be interpreted in a modern therapeutic analytic context as catharsis throwing light and understanding on psychological problems and their roots until one, on the basis of the synthetic and unifying qualities of consciousness, assumes a distinctly unitary mind and self, or individual ego.

Augustine is engaged in the process of submitting his soul to God to be cleansed so that it will be rid of actual sins, although not of temptations to them. Even when sunk deepest into moral and spiritual filth, he has some perception of his state of degradation and some desire to rise out of it. This light grows stronger, and he is cleansed of his philosophical and theological errors. In time he can give the wish to be rid of his sins of the flesh: "Give me continence and chastity", he prays, "but not yet."

But at length grace prevails even over such things, and Augustine's conversion is in one sense a twofold conversion: it is a conversion of the intellect and a conversion of the will.

In another sense it is a threefold conversion: philosophical, moral, and religious. It is a purgation of sins against supernatural truth, the truth revealed by God in this Church, a purgation of sins against natural truths, as found in valid philosophy, and a purgation of sins in the moral order.

As Augustine follows this purgative way, the natural light of intellect grows stronger. When his conversion is completed and he is received into the Church, the supernatural light of sanctifying grace is added to this natural light of reason and intellect. The stronger this twofold light becomes, the closer becomes his union with its source. He is united to God by confession of his sins and by sincere, total, and abiding repentance for them, by belief in all that God has revealed, by the testimony of all that his own powerful mind could discover, by his gratitude for God's goodness, and by his acts of praise for what God is and does.

These three ways, the purgative, the illuminative, and the unitive are not to be thought of as completely separate in time, so to speak, as if the second succeeded entirely to the first, and the third displaced the second. Augustine illustrates the fact that purgation is a lifelong proposition, and he adds a mystical dimension to this process: for him, the light flooding his soul constantly grows stronger and his union with God constantly grows closer and deeper. As he improves his state of perfection, additional mystical graces are given to him so that, through contemplation, he achieves a closer unity. This close unity is characterized by self-renunciation and an intense absorption in the eternal God. This state is occasionally marked by an ecstatic union in which the soul obtains a glimpse of the state of the blessed who live in union with God.

Augustine's threefold confessions of sins, of faith, and of praise, as well as his threefold way of purgation, of light, and of union with God are continually kept in view in the thirteen books which constitute the Confessions. The first nine books describe Augustine's life from his birth through his conversion (Book VIII). In Book X, Augustine presents an intimate portrait of the state of his soul, now that it is transfigured by the grace of baptism. From a psychological point of view, both books are well worth commenting upon.

Augustine struggles with the most difficult psychological problems, involving the nature of will and its acts. He interprets the will as an act rather than as a special power (or faculty) to act or to refrain from acting. Hence, he distinguishes between complete and perfect acts of will and those which are incomplete and imperfect. Thus, for him, there are in man two wills, one of which is not complete:

> "*Mind commands body, and it obeys forthwith. Mind gives orders to itself, and it is resisted...It [Mind] does not give this command in its entirety. For it commands that there be a will, and that this be itself, and not something else. But the complete will does not give the command, and therefore what it commands is not in being. For if it were a complete will, it would not command it to be since the thing would already be in being. Therefore, it is no*

monstrous thing partly to will a thing and partly not to will it, but it is a sickness in the mind. Although it is supported by truth, it does not wholly rise up, since it is heavily encumbered by habit. Therefore, there are two wills, since one of them is not complete, and what is lacking in one of them is present in the other" (VIII, 21).

At a time when he was displeased with his secular life, when he was thirty-two years old, Augustine came under the influence of Ambrose, the Bishop of Milan, and his relationship with Ambrose had a decisive influence on the development of his thought. Dissatisfied with what he saw as the incompleteness of Neo-Platonism and philosophy, he found in Ambrose someone to fill his needs, someone to help him find peace. But there were other influences at work to help bring Augustine to the Church. There was the scene in the garden of his conflict of will over whether or not to renounce the joys of the flesh for the sake of God.

In an agony of irresolution, Augustine threw himself on the ground under a fig tree and wept over his indecision. At that moment, he heard a voice like that of a child chanting Tolle lege "Take up and read! Take up and read!" Seizing a copy of the New Testament, Augustine opened at random and the words that first met his eyes were those of St. Paul to the Romans:

> *"Not in rioting and drunkenness, not in chambering and impurities, not in strife and envying, but put you on the Lord Jesus Christ, and make not provision for the flesh in its concupiscence." (VIII, 29)*

Augustine interpreted this as a divine sign. It eliminated all conflict and doubts in his mind, and he dated his decision to be baptized from that moment during the summer of 386.

In this book, Augustine reveals his motives in writing the Confessions and analyzes the means by which one may achieve the happy life with God:

> *"There is a joy that is not granted to the wicked, but only to those who worship you for your own sake, and for whom you yourself are joy. This is the happy life, to rejoice over you, to you, and because of you: this is it, and there is no other." (X, 32)*

Reflecting upon his own dissatisfaction with himself and his need for God, Augustine undergoes a psychological transformation as a result of God's gift of grace to him.

While Augustine considers himself nothing more than dust and ashes, he is able to know something, however darkly, about God because of the good which God placed in his soul. He states that he will confess what he knows about himself as well as those things he cannot know regarding himself. In revealing what he knows, Augustine declares his total love for God. It is not the pleasures of the senses derived from radiant beauty, fragrant smells, or pleasant melodies that he loves in the act of loving God. It is rather the eternal elements embodied by the light within his soul which can never disappear, that constitute the object of Augustine's love. One can never discover God by his own powers alone. The light of Grace within the soul is freely given to the soul by God:

"Too late have I loved you, O Beauty so ancient and so new, too late have I loved you! Behold, you were within me, while I was outside: it was there that I sought you, and, a deformed creature, rushed headlong upon these things of beauty which you have made. You were with me, but I was not with you. They kept me far from you, those fair things which, if they were not in you, would not exist at all. You

have called to me, and have cried out, and have shattered my deafness. You have blazed forth with light, and have shone upon me, and you have put my blindness to flight!" (X, 38)

It is significant that Augustine approaches his knowledge of God exclusively through his inner experiences. Unlike the thinking of Aquinas centuries later, Augustine must repudiate the Thomistic rationalism which proceeds to prove God's existence from the rational proof of causality. For Augustine, faith must always precede intelligence. Man can never know the truth on his own. God, the source of truth, is present in the soul through the grace of faith. God, therefore, illuminates the soul, providing intellectual light freely and directly to the individual.

Augustine marvels at the memory capacity of the human mind. It is possible to recall images and ideas without utilizing the senses. Knowing these things inwardly is a mystery to Augustine. Yet he does know he possesses this vast and boundless power as a part of his nature. It is even possible to recall in his mind the feelings and emotions of past events which may be relived.

True to the Platonic doctrine of reminiscence, Augustine speculates that there may exist some knowledge unknown to him in his present state, of an earlier state of happiness which all men enjoyed prior to the Original Sin:

> *"Whence and how did these things enter into my memory? How, I do not know, for when I learned them, I did not give credence to another's heart, but I recognized them within my own, and I approved them as true, and I entrusted them to my heart. It was as if I stored them away there, whence I would bring them forth when I wanted them. Therefore, they were there even before I learned them, but they were not in my memory. Where, then, or why, when they were uttered, did I recognize them, and*

say, 'So it is; it is true', if not because they were already in memory, but so removed and pushed back as it were in more hidden caverns that, unless they were dug up by some reminder, I would perhaps have been unable to conceive them." (X, 17).

Finally, in his moments of inner doubt, the dark, deep regions of the subconscious and the mind's powers of self-deception do not escape Augustine's sure analysis as he faces the ever-present temptations which affect him:

"when they are absent, I do not seek them, and when they are present, I do not reject them, but I am prepared to do entirely without them. So do I seem to myself, but perhaps I am deceived. Within me are those lamentable dark areas wherein my own capacities lie hidden from me. Hence, when my mind questions itself about its own powers, it is not easy for it to decide what should be believed. For even what is within it

is for the most part hidden away unless brought to light by some experience." (X, 48).

Many will agree that Augustine is the greatest Christian writer and thinker of all time. In no great mind of Western civilization will we find greater evidence of the synthesis of Greek philosophy, Judaic tradition, and Christian belief than in the works of Augustine. Until the rise of the scholastic Aristotelianism of Aquinas 800 years later, Augustine remained the chief authority of the Church on psychological matters. His insistence on the truth of his contentions based upon the immediate certainty of inner experiences, his stress upon the functioning of the will, his subjective attitude, with its consequent attention to the self and the introspection, as well as his powers of analysis of human behavior also make him a towering figure in the older philosophical psychology concerned with the study of the soul.

R E F E R E N C E S

Augustine (© 400). The Confessions. In R.M. Hutchins (Ed.).

The great books of the western world, Vol. XVIII (pp. 1-125) Chicago: Encyclopedia Britannica.

Battenhouse, R.W. (1955). A companion to the study of St. Augustine. New York: Oxford University Press.

Bourke, V.J. (1945). Augustine's quest of wisdom. Melwaukee: Bruce.

Plotinus (© 270). The six Enneads. In R.M. Hutchins (Ed.).

The great books of the western world, Vol. XVII (pp. 1-360)

Chicago: Encyclopedia Britannica.

Bucke, R.M. Cosmic Consciousness, Dutton Paperback, 1969.

Raphael (1483-1520)

The School of Athens (© 1508-11)

PART TWO

PSYCHOLOGY

AS

Science of Consciousness

Having begun in speculations incidental to the practical problems of mankind and to the search for ultimate truth, psychology ceases to be the science of the soul and, largely due to Descartes (1596-1650), observation and induction supplant metaphysical analysis. Psychology is now understood to be the science of consciousness. The subject of psychology is not man but the mind of man and its contents, and the mind can only be studied by analysis of consciousness.

Descartes starts a quest for absolute knowledge, believing that knowledge is possible because man's mind possesses innate ideas. He poses the body-mind problem which is still being studied currently and the dual aspect of his system becomes the source of two opposite streams of philosophical thought: the mechanistic and the idealistic.

After Descartes, the Empirical School (1588-1776), initiating a radical change in psychological thought, abandons rationalism, holds that experience is the sole source of knowledge, and furthers the study of sensation and perception.

The third most significant philosophical system for psychology, Associationism (1705-1903), adopts the concept of association as a general principle for understanding mind and its content and analyzes the process of association of ideas. Mind is constituted of elements which are identified through introspection.

In the middle of the nineteenth century, psychology emerges as a body of knowledge studied for its own sake and existing in its own right. It looks upon its subject-matter as a part of the world of nature and seeks to explain it in naturalistic terms, observing its material as well as reflecting upon it. In both subject-matter and method, psychology had become empirical; the next step was for it to become experimental.

The name of Wilhelm Wundt (1832-1920), who established a psychological laboratory in Leipzig in 1879, seems to be inevitably linked with the beginning of psychology as an independent science.

The commonly made statement that this was the first psychological laboratory which was founded is not altogether accurate, although the founding is an indispensable point of reference in the important events that led to scientific psychology. It probably was not the first since William James (1842-1910) started almost casually his own laboratory at Harvard in 1875 where he studied sensation. But James was not an experimentalist, and his laboratory did not have the historical importance of Wundt's. Thus, the establishment of the Leipzig laboratory was the outward and visible sign both that psychology had become definitely experimental and that it had become an independent, autonomous science.

The concept of psychology as an experimental science was arrived at due to the influence of many of the philosophers and scientists of the second half of the eighteenth century and first half of the nineteenth century who are well worth mentioning.

Herbart (1776-1841) is among those who influenced Wundt. His mode of thought opposed and dispensed with the "faculty theory" which holds that the soul is endowed with a number of powers – reasoning, remembering, and judging, for example – and explains the specific performances of the mind in terms of the exercise of these faculties.

Herbart's psychology dealt with ideas or mental units somewhat similar to the simple ideas employed by the British associationists and also resembling the monads of Leibniz, and he undertook to explain the most complex mental phenomena in terms of simple ideas (Misiak, 1961).

Mental life is mainly a struggle between ideas,

each of which is active and strives to attain and maintain a place in consciousness and tends to repel all ideas except those with which it is compatible.

This concept made it possible for Herbart to think of mental phenomena in terms of mental mechanics, and also in quantitative terms. Since ideas vary both in time and in force or intensity, psychological material offers two measurable independent variables.

Applying his principles, Herbart wrote mathematical formulas to state the laws of mind, although he did not believe that psychology could ever become experimental. Yet it was partly through his conception of quantitative psychology, especially through the influence of Fechner, that psychology, developed as an experimental science during the half-century following his death. It is interesting to note this fact as an indication of the very gradual manner in which the conception of psychology as science evolved.

Historically, the work of Weber (1795-1878) was of special importance to scientific psychology. A pioneer in physiology, Weber was especially interested in the sense of touch. While he was investigating the relative sensitivity of the cutaneous and muscular senses, he undertook an experiment to determine whether differences in weight could be detected more accurately with or without the active participation of the muscles (Titchener, 1905).

The investigation yielded two discoveries: the first was the direct answer to the main hypothesis: sensitivity to weight is much finer when the muscular sense is included; the second was a discovery that became the starting point of a series of experiments which led straight to experimental psychology and was subsequently formulated as Weber's law.

It was in brief that there was not a simple one-to-one relation between the magnitude of a difference and the subject's ability to perceive it.

For example, if a standard weight of thirty-two ounces was placed on the subject's hand, and the subject was asked to compare with it other weights similarly presented, he was likely to detect an increase in weight when eight or nine ounces – one-fourth of the standard weight – had been added. This value has been called the "just noticeable difference".

But if a standard weight of four ounces was used, an increase in weight could be detected when approximately one additional ounce was added. In other words, a much smaller absolute increment gave rise to a just noticeable difference in the one case than in the other; but again, the difference was about one-fourth of the standard weight. Apparently, the perception of the difference depended not on the absolute size of the difference but on the ratio of the difference to the standard.

The ratio was different, about one to forty when the muscle sense was included, but again fairly constant. And within each of the two sense fields studied, the results for the four persons who served as subjects were roughly the same. Furthermore, the results were confirmed in a subsequent, more carefully controlled experiment.

Weber extended his observations to the discrimination of visual lengths and found that in general, his results confirmed his speculation: it cannot be assumed that there is a simple, literal, point-for-point correspondence between the physical stimulus and the perception of it.

To Weber, this was an interesting physiological fact but no more. However, the discovery was seized upon almost as a revelation by Fechner (1801-1887), who placed it in the very center of the psychological movement (Misiak & Sexton, 1966). Fechner ardently believed that this discovery revealed a connection between the physical and the psychical – an exact mathematical relationship – and a connection of some sort, a unity between the two worlds that Fechner had been seeking long and hard. Fechner literally devoted his life testing what he had called "Weber's law" (Weber himself had not announced it as such):

AR = C, in which R is the stimulus, AR is the just R noticeable difference, and C is the constant, and in so doing worked out methods of investigation that helped to make the science of psychology possible.

Fechner conducted experiments on positive after-images, on degrees of brightness, on visual and tactual distances, believing that if sensation, the point of contact between the physical and the psychical, could be shown to have a definite mathematical relation to the stimulus, the world unity he sought would be established.

He found the constant ratios at least in sufficient quantity and in sufficiently close approximation to ideal requirements to encourage his hopes and his efforts. However, his significance for psychology does not lie in the hoped-for results of his researches but rather in the exact, quantitative experimental procedures he developed in pursuing them.

Fechner himself worked out three of the psychophysical methods, thus called because of his concept of a science of psychophysics dealing with the relationship between the physical and mental worlds.

They were:

1) The method of just noticeable differences, known also as the method of limits.

2) The method of average error, known also as the method of adjustment. Each of these methods comprised a procedure to be followed in the experiment and a mathematical treatment of the collected data.

Fechner faced the most fundamental and persistent problems in experimental psychology: the difficulty of controlling external and internal confounding variables, or replicating the studies, and of refining the quantitative analyses. His techniques were soon utilized by other workers who modified them and applied them to other fields than sensation, and new different techniques were born.

The psychophysical methods themselves aroused the greatest interest. To measure mental processes was a startling innovation; to experiment with them and obtain quantitative results marked the dawn of a new era.

The publication in 1860 of The elements of Psychophysics, the book in which Fechner reported his work and his views, ranks in my opinion with the founding of the Leipzig laboratory in 1879 as one of the outstanding events in the development of psychology, or is perhaps more important since experimental psychology existed long before it housed itself in laboratories.

It may be said that experimental psychology housed itself in other laboratories almost as soon as in the one at Leipzig –in laboratories, furthermore, that did not derive from Wundt. The famous Leipzig laboratory was certainly not the point upon which all pathways leading to experimental psychology converged and from which all subsequent developments took place.

Although Fechner's psychological methods became a regular part of what was rapidly becoming the new science of psychology and are still in use today, they were criticized adversely by none other than William James (1950) in his Principles of Psychology who considered them worthless:

"And everybody praised the duke.

Who this great fight did win.'
'But what good came of it at last?'
Quoth little Peterkin.
'Why, that I cannot tell', said he,
'But'twas a famous victory!" (I, p. 549)

The founding of the new science of psychology was also due to a great extent to Helmholtz (1821-1894), whose researches on the eye and ear functioning rank among the greatest achievements in the field of physics, physiology, and psychology (Misiak & Sexton, 1966).

Helmholtz' studies not only disclosed the enormous complexity of apparently simple psychological processes such as seeing objects and hearing sounds, but at the same time, they brilliantly demonstrated the possibility of studying these processes by the methods of the natural sciences.

It was largely because of his attitude on the side of empiricism (meaning the analysis of fundamental processes which would otherwise have been taken for granted) that Helmholtz demonstrated the possibility of making exact scientific observations on sensation and perception, processes that in his day were regarded as constituting the groundwork of mental life.

As Fechner solidly established both the idea and the practice of measurement in psychology so Helmholtz proved, by his successful researches in sensation and perception, that it was possible to apply exact observation and experimentation to specifically psychological material.

Wundt became the next important figure in the history of psychology who built on the already sizeable amount of scientific work, specifically psychological in character, already at hand, and who gave the final touch that brought the parts together to form a new science.

I strongly believe that Wundt would not have aroused such widespread interest if the way had not been conceptually prepared by his philosophical and scientific predecessors who contributed so substantially to his achievements.

Wundt defined psychology as the science of immediate experience of conscious events; its method was that of systematic introspection and its chief task the analysis of mental processes into conscious elements. (Misiak & Sexton, 1966).

It was in 1858 that Wundt, then Helmholtz' assistant at Heidelberg, first conceived the notion of physiological psychology, a new and experimental psychology that should apply the methods of science to the problems of the Mind.

Reinforced by Fechner's work in psychophysics and Helmholtz's researches in physiological acoustics and physiological optics, Wundt published in 1874 his classic handbook for the new science Grundzüge der physiologishen Psychologie formulating the principles of his system.

According to Boring (1950), Wundt derived the structure of systematic psychology from the British associationists, making sensation the basic element of consciousness.

James Mill had overdone the matter of compounding. The idea of Everything does not still have in it every idea of a thing. There is synthesis. The whole is less, as well as more, than the sum of its parts.

John Stuart Mill had corrected his father on this point. Ideas, he had noted, combine in a kind of mental chemistry, for the parts are lost in the compound which also has properties that were not contained in the parts. Boring contends that Wundt accepted John S. Mill's point of view.

Wundt's book takes up in order the nervous system, the psychic elements (sensation in respect of intensity and quality, and feelings), the formation of the sensory Vorstellungen (perceptions of space, time and intensity, movement and will, and finally the connections of mental processes (association, apperception, consciousness).

Literally, Vorstellung means, of course, presentation but for Wundt, it meant a compound resulting from mental synthesis and thus both perception and idea. His psychology is, therefore, an associationistic sensationism. Until he introduced feelings as a second kind of element, all mind was for him sensations and the results of their synthesis.

After distinction was made between perception and sensation by the later British associationists, and still according to Boring, Wundt, in constructing his system, put into it the sensations as elements of consciousness and the perceptions as complexes of sensations, in that way fixing upon psychology for a long time the notion that the synthesis of elements into complexes is the proper explanation of objective reference and thus of conscious meaning.

But Boring's accounts on Wundt may be questionable. Blumenthal (1980) purports that Boring summarized Wundt's with some of the following points which were either the opposite or were fundamentally different from Wundt's views:

"...Wundt claimed psychology as one of the natural sciences (1950, p. 319); Wundt made introspection the primary method of his laboratory (p.328); Wundt borrowed British associationism and was an elementalist (in the sense of mental chemistry) (p. 329)…"(p. 26).

Contrary to the positivist movement which believed in studying experience devoid of all subjective elements, Wundt specifically placed his interest in these subjective elements. He believed that conscious experience and physiological events cannot be causally related because of their fundamental difference, and that experience is a complex psychological phenomenon produced by a mental synthesis of elements organized into a higher unity (Blumenthal, 1980).

According to Blumenthal (1980) and Denzinger (1979), Wundt's principle of separation between physical and psychological causality kept him in disagreement with the positivist movement, which was for the unity of the sciences and for the reduction of all sciences to physics.

For Wundt, apperception is, of course, the central mechanism of psychological causality but it is not mere attention: it is fundamentally constructive and creative. Hence, to describe elemental psychological processes, Wundt derives "the principle of creative synthesis", meaning that the central volitional process controls all mental constructions whose new products cannot be attributed to outer stimuli. Wundt's view of psychology has been misunderstood, distorted, or described with hostility by many critics. We shall let Wundt, henceforth assigned the title of "Father of psychology", have the last word as he himself summarizes the essence of this psychology:

"Physical causality and psychological causality are polar opposites. The former always implies the postulate of a material substance; the latter never transcends the limits of what is immediately given in mental experience.

'Substance' is a surplus metaphysical notion for which psychology has no use. And this is in accord with the fundamental character of mental life, which I would always have you keep in mind:

It does not consist of the connection of unalterable objects and various states. In all its phases it is a process; an active, not a passive, existence; development, not fixation. The understanding of the basic laws of this development is the primary goal of psychology" (1894, p.495).

Wundt's central concepts of voluntarism, value and psychic causality were rejected as metaphysical by Titchener (1867-1921) who adopted the definition of psychology of the positivist philosophy of science represented by Mach and Avenarius, whose perspective on psychology is described by Danziger (1979):

"Mach and Avenarius rejected the metaphysical dualism of the mental and the physical. As positivists they refused to go beyond what is given in experience; but we do not have two kinds of experience, physical and mental – experience is simply experience. The elements of our experience, however, can be studied from two points of view: We can study relationships among experiences that are independent of the particular biological system to which they belong – in that case, we have the basis for physical science – or we can study relationships among experiences that depend on the particular biological system to which they belong – in which case we practice psychology. The difference between psychology and physical science is therefore not an essential difference; there is no reason why psychology should not aspire to a scientific status comparable to that of the physical sciences." (p.210)

Several young Americans (Hall, Cattell, Angell, etc.) had been among the first students at the Leipzig laboratory. However, it was Titchener – not an American but a young Englishman – who very early imported the new psychology into the United States and became in 1892 Director of the laboratory at Cornell university as well as the official representative in America of the Wundtian tradition.

The new psychology had been described as the science of consciousness. Like Wundt's, Titchener's chief interest was to study how the elements of consciousness combine and he coined his system "structuralism" (Titchener, 1898).

Structuralism held that psychology is human experience studied from the point of view of the experiencing person. The method was still introspection, or self-inspection, and the phenomena must be explained by reference to bodily processes.

The aim of psychology, according to structuralism, (Titchener, 1909) was to investigate the what, the how, and the why of experience or consciousness.

Under what are included the results of introspective analysis of the mental processes. In short, the question of what deals with the content of experience and the problem of its analysis.

The question: How is concerned with the manner in which the various mental processes are related to each other, that is, with the problem of synthesis. The question: Why is concerned with the cause-and-effect relationships between the mental processes and between experience and underlying physiological processes in the nervous system. The first two questions are answered by description; the third seeks explanation.

For Titchener, the analysis of consciousness into its elements resulted in three irreducible components: sensations, images, and affections. Each of these is an element in the sense that it cannot be further broken down by introspective analysis.

Sensations occur in the sights, sounds, smells, tastes, tactual and muscular "feels", and kindred experiences of actually, present physical objects.

Images are the characteristic elements of ideas; they occur in the mental processes that picture, or in some way represent, experiences not actually present, such as memories of the past and imaginings of the future.

Affections are the characteristic elements of emotion; they are found in such experiences as love and hate and joy and sorrow.

But each of these elements can be described in terms of its attributes. All the elements have the attributes of quality, intensity, and duration.

Quality is the most fundamental attribute, which enables the individual to distinguish one experience from another; thus, in the sense of taste, sweet is clearly distinct from sour, and in vision, blue from yellow.

The attribute of intensity is the quantitative aspect of experience; loudness / softness, brightness/dullness, weakness/strength are some of the descriptive terms we utilize to characterize this attribute.

The attribute of duration characterizes how long a sensation, image, or effective state persists in time.

Rejecting Wundt's principle of psychic causality, Titchener states in his Textbook: It is clear that we cannot regard one mental process as the cause of another mental process" (p. 39), and "The explanatory principle for psychology must be looked for beyond, and not within, the world of dependent experience. Physical science, then, explains by assigning a cause; mental science explains by reference to those nervous processes which correspond with the mental processes that are under observation" (p. 41).

It seems clear, therefore, that although Titchener acted as the primary representative of Wundtian psychology in America and enjoyed trading on Wundt's reputation, he misrepresented him to make him more compatible with British empirical associationist traditions (Danziger, 1979) and distorted or fundamentally changed Wundtian thought.

After Titchener's death in 1927, there was no one to carry on the work of structuralism, so the system disappeared from the psychological scene and was superseded by other systems which found it too narrow, too stifling, and too philosophical.

One of these systems was functionalism, which arose at the end of the nineteenth century (1894) at the University of Chicago under the leadership of John Dewey (1859-1952), James R. Angell (1869-1949), and Harvey Carr (1873-1954) and dominated American psychology in the first decade of the twentieth century.

The subject-matter of functionalism was psychical operations and their ends (Angell, 1907). The task of psychology was not to study the structures of the mind but to understand the mind's functions. What was emphasized was no longer the what of consciousness but the what for, leading to the study of motivation, purpose, and goal.

The method of functionalism was principally introspection. Gradually, however, introspection was used less often in research and was replaced by objective methods.

The orientation of functionalistic psychology was essentially Darwinian. The heredity-environment problem; the concept of man as an organism; the study of animal behavior; genetic, comparative, and psycho-physiological studies – all were expressions or results of this orientation.

Adaptation of the whole person to the environment was the principal problem of functionalism. Consequently, research on learning, attention, perception, and intelligence was stressed as significant factors in the adaptive process.

A differentiation of structuralism from functionalism had been given by Titchener (1898) in his Postulates of structural psychology. He acknowledged the contributions of functional psychology, but in his opinion, functional psychology was not pure science, and its methods could not "lead to results of scientific finality". (p. 368).

Titchener thought that only structural psychology was a true science capable of sustaining and preserving the scientific character of psychology and said: "… the best hope for psychology lies … in a continuance of structural analysis". (p. 376)

What Titchener said of functionalism exemplifies his attitude toward other areas: "… there is still so much to be done in the field of analysis… that a general swing of the laboratories towards functional work would be most regrettable" (p. 369).

William James was singled out by Titchener as a typical functionalist in his postulates as he refers to James' "fiat of the Will" or "express consent to the reality of what is attended to" (p. 375):

"This consent… seems a subjective experience sui generis, which we can designate but not define.

We stand here exactly where we did in the case of belief. When an idea stings us in a certain way, and makes another connection with our Self, we say let it be a reality. When it stings us in another way, and makes another connection with ourselves, we believe that it is a reality. To the words 'is' and 'let it be' correspond particular attitudes of consciousness which it is vain to seek to explain…" (James, 1950, II, pp. 568-569).

In the Principles, James assimilated psychology into biology and treated thinking as an instrument in the struggle for life. Mental processes were conceived of as activities. The mind was not an entity, but a functional activity of the organism.

The biological survival value of the mind was stressed; if consciousness had no value, it would not have survived. James saw consciousness as useful because it intervened in the cause-effect sequence, resulting in spontaneity and productivity of the mind.

The functional approach had represented liberation from the constraints of the atomistic psychology of consciousness and a will to expand and move forward to new fields. It corresponded well to the American mentality, which is pragmatic, and to the American temperament, which values action and achievement. In its desire to make psychology useful in the life of the individual and society, functionalism made substantial contributions in the fields of education, business, and industry.

With functionalism, which started as a "school" standing against domination by the Titchenerian, or Wundtian school or system, American psychology passed through a phase of its development in which it brought together and organized many tendencies already in existence, utilizing them so successfully that they passed into general practice.

To treat of psychical activities as well as contents, to think in terms of adaptations and adjustments, to observe psychological processes in relation to their setting, to regard man as a biological organism adapting itself to its environment– all these procedures have been so widely accepted in psychology that they are no longer distinguishable as the property of a single school.

Ultimately, functionalism faded away, its "part" being played, while other schools appeared on the American scene, such as the Gestalt school and particularly behaviorism, which grew out of the functionalist movement.

REFERENCES

Angell, J.R. (1907). The province of functional psychology.

Psychological Review, 14, 61-91.

Blumenthal, A.L. (1980). Wilhelm Wundt and early American psychology: A clash of cultures. In R.W. Rieber & K. Salzinger

(Eds.). Psychology: Theoretical-Historical Perspectives (25-42). New York: Academic Press.

Boring, E.G. (1950). A History of Experimental Psychology (2nd ed.). New York: Appleton-Century-Crofts. (Originally published, 1929).

Danziger, K. (1979). The positivist repudation of Wundt.

Journal of the History of the Behavioral Sciences, 15, 205-230.

James; W. (1950). The principles of psychology (Vols. I and II).

New York: Dover. (Originally published, 1890)

Misiak, H. (1961). The philosophical roots of scientific psychology.

New York: Fordham university.

Misiak, H. & Sexton, V.S. (1966) History of Psychology. New

York: Grune and Stratton.

Titchener, E.B. (1898). The postulates of a structural psychology.

Philosophical Review, VII, 449-465

Titchener, E.B. (1905). Experimental Psychology (Vol. II, Parts I and II). New York: Macmillan.

Titchener, E.B. (1909). A Textbook of Psychology. New York: Macmillan.

Wundt, W. (1894). Vorlesungen über die Menschen –und Theirseele (Translated by Creighton and E. Titchener as Lectures on human and animal psychology). New York: Macmillan. (Originally published, 1892).

PSYCHOLOGY

AS

Human Science

Carl Jung (1875-1961) Mandala

Historically, psychology has begun as the « science of the soul », when all is explained by the existence of a Supreme value outside of man. This concept is later discarded in favor of a « science of consciousness » explained in practical terms when psychology breaks from philosophy. The scientific method applied to this science of consciousness is then found inadequate if psychology is to fulfill its intrinsic potential, and certain thinkers believe that psychology ought to be a human science, or at least different from the natural sciences.

Our scientific civilization has acquired an almost godlike power over the material environment at the expense of certain realms of inner experience that once held the deepest intensity and meaning. As the various forms of religious experience and the intuitive perception of life's meaning have been scientifically undermined, the whole inner aspect of life has been repressed. But now comes a new domain of science that dares to tackle the phenomena of psychological life: this is the science of the inner life of man, a natural history of the evolution of the Self, which Carl Gustav Jung is opening for us.

<u>Ars totum requirit hominem,</u> the art requires the whole man. I believe that Jung's greatest contribution to psychology is the discovery that the existence of that Supreme value lies within the human psyche itself.

Carl Gustav Jung (1875-1961) received his medical degree from the University of Basel, Switzerland, at the turn of the century and had chosen the discipline of psychiatry after having come across von Krafft-Ebing's textbook of psychiatry, which had an indelible effect on him. (Wehr, 1989, p. 17).

Jung states: *"My heart suddenly began to pound. I had to stand up and draw a deep breath. My excitement was intense, for it had become clear to me, in a flash of illumination, that for me the only possible goal was psychiatry. Here alone the two currents of my interest could flow together and in a united stream dig their own bed. Here was the empirical field common to biological and spiritual facts, which I had everywhere sought and nowhere found. Here at last was the place where the collision of nature and spirit became a reality". (Jung, 1963, pp. 108-109).*

In 1900, the medical profession was unsympathetic to the notion of the psyche and considered all nervous disorders as organic in nature. Psychotherapy had developed under the aegis of Sigmund Freud (1856-1939), himself a neurologist, as a separate discipline dealing with neuroses which had no ascertainable physical basis. Freud became interested in the problem of neuroses which, while not organic in origin, could produce physical symptoms (Wehr, 1989, p. 23).

Jung's independent work at the Burghölzli Psychiatric Clinic (Zurich, Switzerland) between 1900 and 1909 proved to him that psychotherapy, the "talking cure", dramatically relieved the suffering of patient who could not be helped by more orthodox methods. At the risk of his academic career in psychiatry, Jung began to publish these findings in The Psychology of dementia praecox (1907), and the content of the psychoses (1908). As a result, he had the opportunity to meet and work with Freud (Wehr, 1989, p. 24).

Freud believed that the etiology of neuroses was the repression or excluding from consciousness of personal impulses or emotions which the conscious mind judged to be uncomplimentary to the view of the self it wished to maintain. These unconscious contents, precisely because they conceal the persons' true nature even from themselves, produce mental and physical manifestations of their existence (Brenner, 1973, p. 80).

Freud's original cure for neuroses resulted from hypnotizing his patients and instructing them to recall the original "trauma" or shock which produced the symptoms (Breuer & Freud, 1955, p.3).

Freud later abandoned the trauma theory as an oversimplification and generalized that neuroses have their origin in some sexual or neurotic conflict which is repressed because the true instincts or emotions are incompatible with conscious attitudes. According to Freud, these repressions are stored in the unconscious, which becomes a kind of "refuse dump" for all kinds of infantile, hostile, and aggressive feelings which the conscious mind refuses to recognize as part of the individual's complete makeup (Jung, 1966, p. 127).

Jung was thoroughly familiar with Freud's work, and he was interested in Freud's theories. In 1913, however, he ended his association with Freud because he could not accept Freud's theory that sexual repression was the exclusive cause of neuroses and that the unconscious had a strictly deleterious nature (Jung, 1933, p. 120).

Jung was also greatly influenced by another early associate of Freud's, Adler (1870-1937), whose heart of teaching was to explore how the social environment influenced the individual's development and personality.

Adler developed a contradictory theory of the origin of neuroses based on what he called a will to power. In this experiential alternative to Freud's Eros theory, a neurosis is not caused by trauma or by infantile sexuality but by the individual's inability to dominate present or future circumstances. (Jung, 1966, p. 53).

As a result of his not being in control of the situation, a person's ego is threatened. To regain control, this neurotic "arranges" to tyrannize, worry, and indirectly exploit others.

Adler's system of Individual Psychology was an attempt to educate the individuals out of their neurotic conflicts by showing them the nature of these neurotic arrangements. Many psychosomatic illnesses would be explained by Adler as an attempt on the part of the "sick" persons to control their family through the family's worry and concern for their present and future health and well-being.

Jung was aware of both Freud's and Adler's conclusions as to the basis of neurosis. Both theories seemed true as they were presented because they explained observable facts and produced cures. Yet, Freud maintained that the ego is dominated by the sexual impulse while Adler argued that the sexual impulse was a subordinate means to the supremacy of the ego (Jung, 1966, p. 35).

One could not hold both theories, then, because they were incompatible with one another. The obvious contrast between successful practice and contradictory theories led Jung to conclude that both Freud and Adler were partially correct, and that their theoretical conflicts were the result of their temperamental and intellectual biases (p. 41).

From this reasoning, Jung generalized that there were two fundamentally different types of personality which he termed extraverted (object-oriented persons) and introverted (subject-oriented persons). Both extraversion and introversion are present in human beings and are considered collectively in Jungian theory as the direction of libido (p. 44).

It must be clarified here that the term "libido" means for Jung psychic energy, which is equivalent to the intensity with which psychic contents are charged, whereas for Freud libido is identified with Eros and distinguished from psychic energy in general (p. 53).

In the introvert, there is a turning inward of libido toward the self. In the extravert, libido is directed outside the self to objects and relationships with objects.

According to Jung, a man who has an extraverted personality is characterized by his outgoing nature, is attracted by people and events, and takes a keen interest in both. This type of person is motivated by external forces, is greatly influenced by the environment, is sociable and self-confident and easily makes himself at home in unfamiliar surroundings (p. 44).

The man with an introverted personality, on the other hand, is characterized by his withdrawal into himself. He is wary of people and of the world about him, and he tends to withhold judgment of both until he has had time to observe his situation. This type of person prefers reflection and solitary pursuits to the frantic pace of group activity. He is unsociable and lacks self-confidence; therefore, he tends to remain as much as possible in situations which are familiar to him.

Each type tends to undervalue the other, since each sees the other as possessing his negative qualities. "The value of the one is the negation of value for the other". (p. 58). Jung makes the interesting observation, however, that these opposite types of personality often marry each other, each providing what the other lacks (p. 55).

Jung concluded that the Freudian attitude is extraverted since it places its center of attention on outside people and events. Adler's attitude, on the other hand, is introverted, for it emphasizes a person's inner attitude in the theory of the will to power (p. 42).

Aware that there are few instances of pure introversion or extraversion, Jung warned of a rigid dependence on types. Man shows not only conformity but also uniqueness. Therefore, the psychology of types must be considered as a generalized explanation. What accounts for the variation of pure types is the primary mode of conscious response.

Jung tells us:

I have found from experience that the basic psychological functions, that is, functions which are genuinely as well as essentially different from other functions, prove to be thinking, feeling, sensation, and intuition.

If one of these functions habitually predominates, a corresponding type results. I, therefore, distinguish a thinking, a feeling, a sensation, and an intuition type. Each of these types may moreover be either introverted or extraverted, depending on its relation to the object... (Gray & Wheelwright, 1945, p.265).

What Jung is saying then is that each person reacts to experiences in terms of four predominant mental functions: sensation, the way we learn of the world through our senses; thinking, the way we understand the world; feeling, the way we evaluate the world around us; and intuiting, the way we come to know about things without tangible, physical evidence.

Each person habitually reacts to the world in one of these ways more than he does in the other three. Thus, certain people will always try to think out, while others will rely on their intuition for an answer to their problems.

The fact that there is a large number of varying personality types in the world is accounted for by the modification of the basic personality type by mental functions, external circumstances, and unconscious individual attitudes.

Jung's theory of types enabled him to pass beyond the partial truths of Eros and the ego interpretations. Both Freud and Adler produced cures because their theories are wholesome correctives for "sick" individuals. But Jung disagreed fundamentally with the hypotheses on which they based their diagnoses (Jung, 1966, p. 40).

Of course, Jung was aware that sexuality and egotism are universally present in every human being, but he resented systems which attempted to define the human psyche as "nothing but" a combination of sex and power drives.

Jung believed that neurosis occurs when either the extraverted or introverted attitude is exaggerated, and a person is unable to integrate the demands of personality and the demands of the external world (p. 166).

Jung's delineation of the introvert and extravert types of personality marked a milestone in the history of psychology. In his book Dimensions of personality (1947) Eysenck shows the kind of results achieved in experimental psychology when these distinctions were adopted, and they are still in current use as descriptive of personality differences.

The fundamental disagreement with Freud and Adler's hypotheses prompted Jung to elaborate a method satisfying deep-seated needs in a new manner, without the necessity of any dogma or belief, and in addition, which could be formulated in terms consonant with the best of modern science; so, he embarked on a tremendous venture, and he chose to work independently of all schools and develop his own system of Analytical Psychology.

Adopting and expanding the methods of Freudian psychoanalysis, Jung developed his own analysis of dreams with the aim to ascertain patterns peculiar to each individual and to understand what set of symbols was consistent in a person's dream.

In his analysis of dreams, Jung drew three conclusions. First, the unconscious content revealed by the dream was not simply instinctual repressions. Second, the unconscious was not simply a passive receptacle for personal repressions: it was an existent with an autonomous force of its own, able to direct its images in its own way. Third, the unconscious produces spontaneous images which extend beyond the personal experience of the individual (Jung, 1966, pp. 127, 128 and 183).

If Freud and Adler were correct as to the passive nature and the repressed content of the unconscious, then when the contents of the unconscious have been brought to consciousness and the neurosis has been worked out, the unconscious continues to produce spontaneous, apersonal image. Jung then sought to explain the source of these dreams and images (p. 128).

It was Jung's belief that there is a further dimension to the unconscious, which he termed the "collective" or impersonal unconscious. The repressed and forgotten events of a person's life are stored in the "personal" unconscious. The experience of the race of man is possessed by each individual in his collective unconscious. It is from this level of man's being that primordial images and dream symbols arise (p. 66).

In interpreting his patient's dreams, therefore, Jung based himself on that collective unconscious and on his study of the lore of primitive man.

It is a known fact that while the collective unconscious cannot be empirically established, it can be indirectly observed in the works of genius, art, and insanity. Before Jung, artists, and pioneers, in giving expression to the underlying movements of the time, had turned to the unconscious in their search for a deeper reality than the dubious realities of the senses and the reason and felt that this reality was to be found only in the depths of the psyche of man. Also, the more than coincidental similarities of the myths and religious rituals which are found in all cultures indicate that the collective unconscious can be traced through them.

Jung believed that the collective unconscious functions independently of the conscious ego. The collective images, which Jung called "archetypes", cannot be summoned at will, but rather force themselves upon the mind with a seeming will of their own. The analogy which Jung suggests is society's relation to the individual. Just as we recognize that society is outside of the individual, so also, we can acknowledge that there is a collective unconscious which extends beyond the personal unconscious and the conscious ego. The relation between the individual psyche and the collective psyche is similar to this relationship between the individual and society (p. 145).

Just as society makes demands which are opposed to personal interests, so also the collective unconscious contradicts the personal ego. In so far as human brains are similar in their functioning, these functions are collective (p. 155).

Thus, personality represents the way in which our consciousness and personal unconscious have become unique. The collective unconscious represents the deep-rooted, inherent thought patterns of a specific race or a portion of humanity, which transcend the contents of the individual psyche.

Among others, the merit of Analytical Psychology, which is a dynamic one, has been to switch the emphasis from studying disease to working toward health.

The aim of Analytical Psychology is the achievement of self-realization or individuation.

Jung stressed the difference between individuation and individualism. According to him, individualism is the view which emphasizes the unique peculiarities of the individual as opposed to collective qualities of mankind in the personal individual, making him the unique person he is (p. 173).

Self-realization is possible only when there is a state of equilibrium between the conscious and the unconscious elements in man. If a man attempts to live by his reason alone, the unconscious resents being ignored and rebels. If this shadow side of man's existence is disavowed, man fashions for himself an image which he presents to the external world. Jung calls this image "persona" from the Greek for mask (Jung, 1966, p. 157).

Although the persona seems to underscore the individuality and uniqueness of the individual, the persona is, in truth, a collective phenomenon. It is composed of characteristics which might equally well belong to anybody, but each individual's persona is different because each man chooses different components to make up his mask (p. 158).

The persona is a necessary part of the personality for it is through the persona that we relate to the outer world. The danger of the persona arises when a man identifies himself with the role he plays. While this kind of person may appear to be an individual, he is really not seeing reality as it exists. He has not achieved the conscious-unconscious integration which would make him a true, "complete" individual.

Analytical Psychology attempts to take off the mask. By acknowledging what his psyche really consists of, a man must admit to himself that the social role he has fashioned does not take into account the ways things actually exist.

As he delves into the recesses of his personal unconscious, man discovers the elements of his personality which he has discarded in order to keep his mask intact. When he has made an attempt at understanding, the mask begins to disappear. The power of the persona is lessened as a man is able to acknowledge the "dynamic equilibrium" that exists between his conscious and his unconscious. He is able to free himself from this domination by the unconscious archetype by incorporating the demands of his unconscious within his conscious mind.

Jung viewed the psyche, or total personality, as self-regulating and constructed in terms of complementary opposites. As was apparent earlier in this paper, Jung recognized also that when libido flows into introversion, it is withdrawn from extraversion. The same principle of complementarities holds in the relation of the conscious to the unconscious and one of its aspects has been delineated by Jung in terms of masculine/feminine polarity. It was Jung's belief that each man possesses an unconscious female complement, called "anima", and that each woman possesses an unconscious male complement, called "animus" (p. 188).

The problem man faces in his attempt to integrate his personality is to come to terms with the complex relationship between the persona and the anima, i.e., the masculine image which is projected and the feminine image which is inherited. These opposites create the tension which is the basis for self-mastery.

Primitive cultures seemed to be able intuitively to grasp the nature of this tension and the need to reconcile it. Thus, they formulated elaborate initiation and puberty rites which symbolically severed man from the hold of the archetypal anima. After the rites had been performed, man was free from the unconscious and incorporated within his conscious personality (Campbell, 1988, p. 87).

So, man must be able to separate what he is (self) from how he appears to others (persona), and what he instinctively desires (personal unconscious) from the attraction of the archetypal images (collective unconscious).

While the anima and the animus are residents of the collective unconscious, they come to man's consciousness in his dreams and fantasies. It is there that they can be studied, and that man can learn of the makeup of his unconscious. Each bit of knowledge a man gains in this direction frees him from the blind control of his unconscious and puts him one step further toward self-realization (Jung, 1966, p. 210).

When a person recognizes the existence of an archetype within himself, it is very important that he does not identify himself with the archetype. Such identification on the unconscious level is just as harmful as an identification with the persona on a conscious level (p. 152).

In order to avoid the pitfalls of identification with one's conscious or unconscious nature, one must find a suitable half-way point which allows the natural dynamic equilibrium of the psyche to continue uninterrupted. One must discover a new center of personality, which Jung called the "self" (p. 177).

It must be understood that the self is different from the ego, which Jung believed to be the center of consciousness. To attempt to have the ego as the center point is to try to control the unconscious by the conscious. The self takes into account the wishes of both the conscious and the unconscious. It is the means whereby the various parts of personality are unified, and it acts as a balance point for stability and equilibrium.

Thus, self-realization comes about when we are ready to accept ourselves as we really are. Neither side of man's nature is striving for supremacy. Each is acting as a complement of the other. There are no unnatural pockets of energy, no "complexes" that hinder the flow of energy back and forth between the conscious and the unconscious. Man can function in the modern world without denying the existence and influence of the past.

Another of Jung's towering pioneering achievements has been to bring the religious experience to psychology. Jung demonstrated that the unconscious mind is the source of man's religious attitude. Herein lie the eternal symbols that man has used throughout his history to express his feelings on life, death, and immortality. These symbols of the unconscious are made known to man's conscious mind through his dreams which can make his life meaningful and understandable (Jung, 1938, p. 27).

Jung presented a view of God as being within man. He pointed out that "… What one could almost call a systematic blindness is simply the effect of the prejudice that the deity is outside man" (Jung, 1938, p. 72).

This "spatial" location of where we believe our God exists makes a difference in a man's personality. If man sees his God as "out there", then his personality is split, and he is forever searching for his whole self. On the other hand, if he believes his God is "in here", then his personality is integrated, and he is a whole human being.

The basic conflict between Jung and Freud encompassed Freud's hostility to ideas of spirit. Jung believed that the basic source of neurosis in adults is the loss of spiritual frame of reference. This spiritual emptiness is not restricted to neurotics but constitutes the general problem of contemporary culture. It is for this reason that psychotherapists have replaced the clergy as the spiritual advisors of our age.

Commenting on Freud's inability to understand the religious experience as he over-emphasizes the pathological aspect of life, Jung comments:

What Freud has to say about sexuality, infantile pleasure, and their conflict with the "principle of reality", as well as what he says about incest and the like, can be taken as the truest expression of his own psychic make-up. He has given adequate form to what he has noted in himself.

For my part, I prefer to look at man in the light of what in him is healthy and sound, and to free the sick man from that point of view which colors every page Freud has written.

Freud's teaching is definitely one-sided in that it generalizes from facts that are relevant only to neurotic states of mind; its validity is really confined to those states. Within these limits, Freud's teaching is true and valid even when it is in error, for error also belongs to the picture, and carries the truth of a true avowal. In any case, Freud's is not a psychology of the healthy mind. (Jung, 1933, pp. 116-117).

When Jung looks at the situation of modern man, he views him not as an average person but as a highly conscious figure who faces the unknown future as the heir of the whole history of mankind.

Since every step toward self-consciousness is a separation from submersion in the unconsciousness observable in primitives, modern man is preeminently an egocentric and solitary individual. His highly differentiated consciousness lives in the present and the values and ideals of the past seem irrelevant to him. He is modern because his self-consciousness has brought him to the edge of a world which he has outgrown and discarded (Jung, 1933, p. 197).

The truly modern man is basically "unhistorical" in a psychological sense. His self-consciousness estranges him not only from the average man, but also from the traditions and institutions which offer existential meaning to the ordinary person. The modern consciousness is not hostile toward the past but sadly aware that its solutions are not relevant to him. The vague sense of guilt at not being at peace with the world motivates him individually to supply meaning through his own creative ability. Thus, the efficient, intelligent, and creative modern consciousness – with its sense of isolation and meaninglessness – must be distinguished from the pseudo-modern individual who is personally incompetent and disloyal to the traditions of his past. The temptation of modern consciousness is to view its own sense of despair as the end product of human evolution (pp. 198-199).

Jung interprets the modern psyche as a manifestation of the principle of enantiodromia (conversion into the opposite) (p. 204).

The insecurity, uncertainty, and skepticism of modern man is seen as a necessary stage in the discovery of new spiritual ideals which make life worthwhile.

The most important sign that man is making this transition is the current fascination with the nature of the human psyche.

Just as the individual recognition of the complementary natures of a person's conscious and unconscious aspects is important on a personal level, so on a social level one can see that the extraverted, naturalistic, and technological outlook of western civilization is being reciprocally influenced by the introverted, mystical, and contemplative outlook of eastern culture (Jung, 1976, p. 487).

The modern man will not abandon his egocentricity even though it is one cause of his neuroses. He wants to experiment with every element of his personality, to test the meaning which every value has for him and to discover the secrets of life.

The intellectual tradition of the West has promoted blind faith and blind rationalism for so long that modern man can no longer believe in either. He seeks a new synthesis of life to give meaning to his existence.

Brenner, C. (1973). *An elementary textbook of psychoanalysis.*

New York: Anchor Books.

Breuer, J. & Freud, S. (1955). Studies on hysteria. The standard edition of the complete psychological works of

Sigmond Freud, 2, 1-305. London: Hogarth Press. (Originally published, 1895).

Campbell, J. (1988). The power of myth. New York: Doubleday.

Gray H. & Wheelwright, J.B. (1945). Jung's psychological types, including the four functions. Journal of general psychology, 33, 265-284.

Jung, C.G. (1933). Modern man in search of a soul. (Translated by W.S. Dell and C.F. Baynes). New York: Harcourt Brace

Jovanovich.2nd

Jung, C.G. (1938). Psychology and religion. New Haven: Yale

University Press.

Jung, C.G. (1963). Memories, dreams, reflections. New York:

Pantheon Books.

Jung, C.G. (1966). Two essays on analytical psychology (2 nd ed.),

(Translated by R.F.C. Hull, Bollingen Series XX). Princeton,

N.J.: Princeton University Press.

Jung, C.G. (1976). The portable Jung (J. Campbell, Ed.). New York: Penguin Books.

Wehr, G. (1989). An illustrated biography of C.G. Jung

(Translated by M.H. Kohn). Boston: Shambhala.

CONCLUSION

From the science of the soul to human science, pointing to spiritual science, it seems that we have come full circle. In the first part the soul stands prominent and in the last part seems to claim again its due, as if a gap had to be filled. This means that psychology cannot be reduced to a discipline modelled after the physical sciences, essentially based on sense observation and experimentation, ignoring the supersensible. Both scientist and borderline mystic, Carl Jung gives a note of hope for the spiritual development of humanity:

> *"Within the last decade there have been many references from varied sources to the fact that the western world stands on the verge of a spiritual rebirth, that is, a fundamental change of attitude toward the values of life. After a long period of outward expansion, we are beginning to look within ourselves once more. There is very*

general agreement as to the phenomena surrounding this increasing shift of interest from facts as such to their meaning and value to us as individuals, but as soon as we begin to analyze the anticipations nursed by the various groups in our world with respect to the change that is to be hoped for, agreement is at an end and a sharp conflict of forces makes itself felt..." Carl Gustav JUNG – *Modern Man in search of a soul.*

Along the same lines, the French writer and statesman, André Malraux said: "The twenty-first century will be spiritual, or it will not be".

Marc Chagall (1875-1965) United Nations-Stained Glass Window

The experiences and influences which have most shaped my interest in the human sciences are multiple. In retrospect I can single out some of the salient milestones which have marked my life and career.

The most important I can think of are, first, my encounter with Humanistic thinkers and philosophers of the Renaissance, that is to say with people who had a high idea of man and his destiny.

Humanist scholars were convinced of man's freedom, of the power of the spirit and intelligence as part of an evolutionary and transformative force. They praised man in terms of the positive capacities generously granted him by God when He created man in his own image. They held the idea that Nature seeks to realize the perfection of which it is capable, and that man, as part of Nature, is a link between the intellectual and the sensible world. With God above him and animals, plants, and matter below him, he is free to progress toward the fulfillment of his potential toward perfection.

The humanistic idea of perfection included both mind and body, contemplation, and action, the good of the soul and the elevation of intelligence, as well as physical beauty and health. This was a holistic vision which had a great impact on my thought during my formative years.

No less important to me was the transcendental vision of the mystics, those who are experiencing God, and cosmic consciousness. The book by Richard Maurice Bucke, entitled "Cosmic Consciousness" came to confirm the idea I had already nurtured, and made me aware of a greater truth, another reality, which had to be experienced, explored, and explained. I came to believe that the "visible" the "ordinary" world did not represent the limits of human nature and that man's destiny is to evolve toward some higher state of consciousness; that we are not just limited personalities operating in a limited social world but can view ourselves as more cosmic and more spiritual beings. Then, guided by the principles and ideals embodied in the United Nations Charter, I joined the Organization in New York where I worked in different capacities, namely as an officer in the Department of Legal Affairs. In this forum of all Nations, where the work setting is a microcosm, I had the privilege to work on the staff of Secretary-General Dag Hammarskjöld, a towering figure, truly serving the ideals and principles of the UN in his unique function which he regarded as his true vocation and for which he was specially gifted.

It was an unforgettable experience to work with such an outstanding chief and leader as well as a spiritual teacher. His intellect, courage, and stamina were legendary as was the self-discipline he imposed on himself in order to master the tremendous load of work he had to assume in the United Nations. To him the Secretary-Generalship was the greatest of blessings. In the performance of his duties, he provided an exhilarating spectacle of principle and mind in action. At the same time his humor, genuine simplicity and kindness made him a wondrous boss. His boundless energy was extraordinary by any standard. In situations of crises, he would work endless hours with very little sleep and no apparent fatigue and spurred everyone around him to do the same, as I have personally experienced in the Congo.

His virtuosity in the fields of law, politics, logic, economics, and finance were comprehensive and his power of concentration, his penetrating analytical mind, enabled him to master quickly any complex problem. He relied very little on notes or references and could dictate or deliver extemporaneously long speeches or reports. For such a busy man his office was meticulously neat; to my great astonishment, his desk rarely had more than one or two pieces of paper on it.

Besides his unusual, somewhat awesome intellectual capacities he was recognized for his integrity, disinterestedness, and purity of intention, even by those with whom he frequently and strongly disagreed.

What impressed me most was his religious and mystical insights. Religion for him was a dialogue of his own with God. As he wrote in his book "Markings" "Faith is a state of mind". He was searching for a spiritual meaning which transcended the world. He believed in the vocation of the United Nations; he believed in the advent of a New Human Order, and he hoped that the UN would gradually become a constitutional instrument recognized and respected by all nations. He was a true humanist, a remarkable man, a great Secretary-General, totally dedicated to his mission.

Still while at the UN I joined a spiritual group under the leadership of a Jesuit priest, who was Director of the UN Division for Natural Resources.

He was a geologist with extensive experience in paleontology and had been with Teilhard de Chardin in China. It was he who introduced me to the philosophy of Teilhard and I became overwhelmed with the Teilhardian liberating vision of the universe and of the transcendental evolution of man which so radically departed from narrow dogmas to embrace a cosmic dimension. It was comforting to think in terms of mind pervading matter, of spiritual energy enhancing the evolution of the world to higher consciousness, from the "biosphere" to the "noosphere".

At about the same period I was also introduced to Religious Science, Branch of the New Thought Movement, whose founder was Ernest Holmes, a self-made man and philosopher/spiritual teacher who had also a strong conviction of the unity of the universe and of the power of mind over matter. I then became better conversant with the nature of Mind and the role of the subconscious. I was interested in the power of faith and spiritual healing, that is, the influence of thoughts on the body and the interaction between body and mind. I became a licensed practitioner of Religious Science, counseling, and helping people solve their problems and conflicts. This led me to realize that I should know more about psychology and get formal academic training in this fascinating field which had become my dearest, compelling life endeavor.

So, while working full-time in a very demanding position at the UN, I embarked in the study of psychology, completing my B.A. and M.A. degrees and taking 33 credits as a matriculated student in a doctoral program in neuropsychology. Strongly believing in the necessity of life-long education, my aim was to acquire knowledge at the highest level in my new field and to familiarize myself with the research methods needed to investigate brain-behavior relationships.

I became convinced however, that the study of psychology could not use the same approach and methods for human and nonhuman subjects and could not disregard the spiritual dimension. As Stanley Krippner puts it in an interview given to the Science of Mind Magazine (March 1987): "Human beings represent body, mind, emotions, and spirit – four basic elements that are constantly interacting and working together. If a person is undertaking an intensive study of human beings and neglects some of these aspects, the data are not going to represent the totality of what is being studied." (p. 12).

These are some of the significant events in the evolution of my thought and interest toward the human sciences and humanistic psychology. Psychology cannot be limited to behaviorism or psychoanalysis and must be holistic, finding its place in the "Second Copernican Revolution" and bringing more wisdom and happiness in this world.

A N N E X

Considering the influence of Neo-Platonism on both St Augustine and Carl Jung, it is appropriate to quote Plotinus' seminal letter to Flaccus.© 260

PLOTINUS' LETTER TO FLACCUS

You ask me to tell you how we know, and what is our criterion of certainty. To write is always irksome to me. But for the continued solicitations of Porphyry, I should not have left a line to survive me. For your own sake and for your father's my reluctance shall be overcome.

External objects present us only with appearances rather than knowledge. The distinctions in the actual world of appearance are of import only to ordinary and practical men. Our question lies with the ideal reality that exists beyond appearances.

How does the mind perceive these ideas? Are they without us, and is the reason, like sensation, occupied with objects external to itself? What certainty would we then have – what assurance that our perception was infallible? The object perceived would be a something different FROM the mind perceiving it. We should have then an image instead of a reality. It would be monstruous to believe for a moment that mind is unable to perceive Ideal Truth exactly as it is, and that we had not certainty and real knowledge concerning the world of intelligence.

It follows therefore that this region of Truth is not to be investigated as a region external to us, also only imperfectly known. It is within us. Here the objets we contemplate and that which contemplate are identical – both are thoughts. The subject cannot surely know an object different from itself. The world of ideas lies within our intelligence. Truth, therefore, is not the agreement of our apprehension to an external object with the object itself. It is the agreement of the mind with itself. Consciousness therefore is the sole basis of certainty. Thc mind is its own witness. Reason sees in itself that which is above itsel as its source; and again, that which is below itself as still itself once more.

Knowledge has three degrees: opinion, science, illumination. The means or instrument of the first is sense, of the second dialectic of the third, intuition. To the last I subordinate reason. It is absolute knowledge founded on the identity of mind knowing with the object known.

There is a raying out of all orders of existence, an external emanation from the ineffable one. There is again a returning impulse, drawing all upwards and inwards towards the center where all came. Love, as Plato in the Banquet beautifully says is child of poverty and plenty. In the amorous quest of the soul after the good, lies the painful sense of fall and depravation. But that love is blessing, is salvation, is our guardian genius; without it the centrifugal law would overpower us and sweep our souls out far from their source toward the cold extremities of the material and the manifold.

The wise man recognizes the idea of the Good within him. This he develops by withdrawal into the holy place of his own soul. He who does not understand how the soul contains the beautiful within itself seeks to realize beauty without by laborious production. His aim should be rather to concentrate and simplify and so to expand his being; instead of going out into the manifold, to forsake it for the One, and so to float upwards towards the Divine Fount of being whose stream flows within him.

You ask, "How can we know the Infinite?"

I answer, "Not by reason". It is the office of reason to distinguish and define. The Infinite therefore cannot be ranked among its objects.

" You can only apprehend the Infinite by a faculty superior to reason, by entering into a state in which you are your finite self no longer – in which the divine essence is communicated to you. This is ecstasy. It is the liberation of your mind from its finite consciousness. Like only can apprehend like, when you thus cease to be finite, you become one with the Infinite. In the reduction of your soul to its simplest self, its divine essence, you realize this union, this identity.

`But this sublime condition is not of permanent duration. It is only now and then that we can enjoy this elevation (mercifully made possible for us) above the limits of the body and the world. I myself have realized it but three times as yet, and Porphyry hitherto not once. All that tends to purify and elevate the mind will assist you in this attainment and facilitate the approach and the recurrence of these happy intervals. There are, then, different roads by which this end may be reached. The love of beauty which exalts the poet; that devotion to the One and that ascent of science which makes the ambition of the philosopher, and that love and those prayers by which some devout and ardent soul tends in its moral purity towards perfection. These are the great highways conducting to that height above the actual and the particular, where we stand in the immediate presence of the Infinite, who shines out as from the deeps of the soul.

[quoted from R. Bucke's Cosmic Consciousness]

9 798888 753409